Reflections

REFLECTIONS
of quiet times

Helen DesChene

Illustrations by Jill Renee Marquis

GOLDEN QUILL PRESS
PUBLISHERS SINCE 1902
PRESCOTT, ARIZONA

GOLDEN QUILL PRESS
Prescott, Arizona
© Helen DesChene, 1999
All Rights Reserved
Library of Congress
Card Catalog Number:
99-070327
I.S.B.N. 0-8233-0513-9
Printed in the United States of America

Dedicated...

to all my friends both old and new...
who have repeatedly asked "when?"

I thank you...
and give to you this bit of nostalgia.

Your interest and caring has lifted my spirits...
and blest my life.

Contents

Preface

Having grown up in Saugus, Massachusetts, I had always been involved in church and music, but not until we moved to Topsfield had the Lord jolted me with such an overwhelming force. Poetry tumbled out of my pen as it never had before and my episode with cancer gave - everything I had taken for granted - greater importance. The trees became much greener, the flowers brighter and friends more special.

I urge you to be aware of some things as I see them. Such gifts God gives us!

Let me take you to some of my favorite places: to our log cabin in the mountains, to the seashore, maybe to Holland, and let me tell you about my Lord...

"May God's peace be in us."

REFLECTIONS
of quiet times

Helen DesChene
Illustrations by Jill Renee Marquis

Rustling Taffeta

A crow flew by –
    Quite eloquent – in black
To perch high in the pine tree
    By my door

And from his lofty perch
    Surveyed the yard.
What was he thinking-
    Of the day in store?

Then - off he pushed
    Folding his feathered garb
Like taffeta. It rustled
    As he passed -

And - thought I
    of one lady - long ago -
A fleeting moment,
    Memory of the past.

Every experience God gives us...
Every person He puts in our lives
Is the perfect preparation for the
    Future...That only He can see!

Our Mountain Pond

Pale blue and fading fast
    the summer sky...
Held up by puffy clouds
    of white and cream.
The sun slips now
    behind the distant hills
And sudden shades
    of apricot are seen
To color softly
    all the bits of cloud...
So strong the color
    takes my breath away...
Intensifying...shouting
    as it comes,
Reflecting round us now
    the end of day.
We gasp...
    the magic splendor of it all!
Then...it is gone
    as quickly as it came.
Soft silence...now
    pervades the shadowed shore
With evening...on
    the waters of our pond.

My World

All my world was washed
    by God - last night.
The remnant of an early
    autumn rain

Left puddles on the path
    and cleaned the air
Until I found the sun
    shine warm again.

The clouds – hung heavy
    on the distant hill
Made dull the sky
    and too – the distant shore.

Now waters sparkle
    and the skies are blue
And warm reflections
    cheer my open door.

In Season Walk

Short months ago
I found my path adorned
With dainty rose –
With apricot – and cream.
Soft petals of
Another place and time –
A warmer day –
A summer day –
A dream.........

And now – October
Pads the trail I wander
With bits of scarlet–
Yellow – rust – and gold.
Crisp leaves lay
Over-lapping one another,
And choosing one –
My fingers ache
With cold.........

Moonbeams

Soft mist, on shafts of light
Invade my woods...

The Product
Of a full October moon...

The quietness profound
Has beckoned me

At midnight. Magically
I'm upward drawn...

Ethereal, these moonbeams
And so strong!

Envisioned now
As tho' t'were but a dream...

This magic moment.
It shall linger long...

Encroached, 'mid giant shadows
It would seem...

And all too soon
My bit of magic...gone

But...ne'er forgotten...
Shared...with God alone!

Solitude

Sun - shines among the silent pines
And casts its shadows
On each mound of gleaming snow.

In awe – I stare at such a sight.
I look around – no one to share –
Or care –
That I am struck with awe –
At what I've found!

The sky is blue – beyond belief.
I stand quite still.
I hear no sound.

Such beauty fills my very soul
And feels the Presence of my God!
The air is sharp.
My heart is warm
And spirits soar to heights profound!

Deer Prints

Oh precious deer
    Who pass my way,
Distinctive tracks
    Give you away,
For you have entered
    My domain.
My shrubs will never
    Look the same!
Here in my window
    Long I've stood
To watch you forage
    For your food.
You leave your footprints
    In the snow
And silently
    You come and go.
Elusive creatures
    Of the storm,
Who disappear
    When days turn warm.

A Friend

Soft memories
Invade a dreaming space.
  The tears of sentiment
  Stream down my face.
Surrounded we
In quiet fantasy
  Of make-believe
  And what we longed to be.

Descriptive, dreaming,
Elegant was she.
  I idolized
  The time she spent with me.
No one can take
Our dreams of yester-year,
  For always, in my heart,
  My friend is near.

Crystal

The branches, crystal glaze
    encased in ice...
Sway to and fro and creak
    rebelliously.

It's nearly Spring. Enchantment
    fills my wood
And mesmerized... it thrills
    the heart of me.

A Change In The Weather

The sun is shining brightly
On the bird-bath...full of ice.

The puddle's etched in ripples
Where it's frozen once or twice.

Today is cold and windy...
Tomorrow may be hot...

And crocuses...now wonder
Should they wake up yet...or not?

Early Easter

We burn the limbs of winter – and
We rake the lawn with cheer,

Replace the coats and over-shoes
With brighter, lighter gear

When suddenly a warning comes
And then – a foot of snow!

It's April now – and Easter's
Nearly here – tho' don't you know

It's awfully hard to think of
Dainty dress and Easter hat.

How can we have an egg hunt
When the yard is full of that?

And drifting banks of white stuff
Are too deep to even blow!

It's hard to think of Easter
When we're wallowing in snow!

Spring Snowflakes

How silently they drift
    And silent lay

Upon the blossoms
    Of an early Spring.

They disappear as quickly
    As they come,

But one soon cools another
    So the lawns

Receive their magic
    Carpeting of white.

A winter wonder
    On an April earth

Says "Not quite yet!"
    And it's an awesome sight,

The last sweet flakes
    That fall, in early Spring!

Spring Song

Winds whisper
In the dawn of early morn
When air is cool
And sun is barely up
   And from the mountain-top
   Still white with snow,
   A freshness with it
   Over-flows my cup.
The may flower
And trillium are gone
And in their stead
The lady-slippers pink
   Now shock the woodland
   Brown in fallen leaves.   A pair of orioles
   Each fragile bloom   Work frantically
   A miracle...I think.   To pull some threads
                       Of rope to make a nest.
                          Where will you hang
                          The pocket that you weave
                          So carefully
                          To cradle baby...best?
                       I can but thrill
                       The joyfulness of Spring
                       When from the remnants
                       Of a winter...long,
                          All nature comes alive
                          To burst in bloom
                          While bird and frog and beetle
                          Join...in song.

April Showers

Our April showers come in May,
Our blooms of May, in June,
    Then winter snows have vanished
    And the summer...here too soon,
        Now where pray tell is springtime
        When the seasons get in tune?

Robins

The sky is dull
    And eerie mist
        Has dressed the lawn in dew

And though we care not
    Venture out
        We see, the robins do.

In fluffy
    Happy splendor
        They strut across the lawn

And know full well
    T'will soon provide
        Some worms to lunch upon!

"Quiet Time"

I quick arise
   At break of dawn
      To watch...with awe
         The morning come.

The sky is soft,
   The air is still.
      The sun is up...
         On rock and rill.

The pond...a mirror
   Of each tree.
      I gulp the view...
         I seek to fill

My head with
   Memories...alas...
      Of here and now...
         Then...it is past...

The noise of morn...
   The rippling breeze...
   The stirring sound
      Of wind and trees

      Obliterate...

      Tranquility...

Stone-Walls

I love stone-walls.
    They have so much to tell –
That separated roadway
    From the wood
And there divided cattle
    As they stood
Caressing tuft of grasses
    Green and good.

I love stone-walls.
    They tell a story old –
Of woodlands cleared.
    Where else to put the stone
But bordering each field
    He cleared, alone
And neatly piled in rows.
    They are not gone,

Encrusted with
    A macramé of moss
And bound together
    Often with a vine,
Some tumbling now
    Irregular the line,
With gate, still hanging
    Careless faded sign.

Long walls – that prove
    The laboring of man
On which – perhaps
    His hefty scythe was hone.
I love stone – walls.
    They guard a plot – alone.
Cold stone – that warms
    The winding road to home.

Quiet Road-Side

A country walk
    Reveals a multitude
        Of treasures that
            Cannot be seen by car.

Soft sounds the hard
    Packed gravel...to allow
        The call of bird
            And nature...from afar.

While there...among
    The asters, golden rod
        Protected by the
            Thorns of berry-bough.

Black, juicy berries
    Shining in the sun
        Hang heavy...and await
            The picking now.

With both my hands
    I pluck...to overflow
        The succulence of nature
            As I stroll.

The juicy sweetness
    Thrills my palate...and
        The quietness of nature
            Fills my soul.

Morning Walk

Oh soft and gentle breeze
		Of early Spring
That fills my heart
		With happy birds to sing
And treats the air
		With fragrances unsung.
With lilting step
		Today...I'm feeling young!

How Still

From my canoe
   The quiet is profound...
    No ripple mars
      The mirror of my pond...

The woods are still...
   There is no breeze...
    One blue-jay screeches
     In the trees...

One squirrel scolds him...
   That is all...
    And one acorn...
     I hear it fall...

"My Treasure"

I have
A secret garden
And it winds
A wood-land path.
It's very short – around a bush
And all too soon I'm back –

But down my little pathway
There's a multitude of dreams
Caught in clumps of columbine
And shadows – so it seems.

Through lily–of–the–valley
And my blue forget-me-not
Jack-in-the-pulpits flourish
In my very special spot.

A patch of dainty violet
Beneath a craggy pine –
A moment, lost in solitude –
God's treasures – they are mine.

A *Summer Storm*

The summer sky
Has very slowly darkened
And imminent, it threats a summer storm.

Hot sun is pushed aside
By cooling dampness
And waves replace the ripples on my pond.

The daylight fades
And wind torments the branches.
The birds protest the evening comes too soon.

The cabin beckons
Bright and warm protection
While softly cries a solitary loon.

White shards of lightning
Pierce the black of evening
And torrents beat upon my window pane.

The shutters rattle
And the thunder bounces
And rolls from hill to hill and back again.

Yet soon, amid
The turbulence and clatter,
The onslaught of a pounding summer rain

Can bathe the woods
Of dust and broken branches
With promise that the sun will shine again.

Early Morn

Hunched over
    In the sun of early morn,
Back arched, against
    The chilling mountain wind,

The sun is sharp
    And blinding to my gaze
That I near miss
    The loon that's gliding by.

Lo thinking he
    The only soul awake
Upon the quiet
    Of our mountain pond,

I share with him
    The sunny solitude
Of early morning
    Autumn leaves
        That fall.

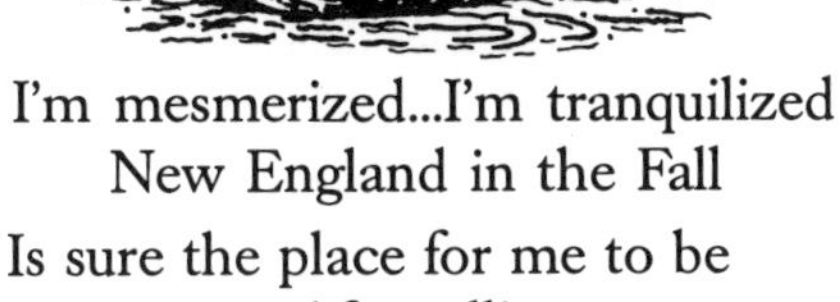

I'm mesmerized...I'm tranquilized
    New England in the Fall
Is sure the place for me to be
        After all!

Retirement!

Peaceful, our retired way
And languidly, I have to say
No need the rise at break of day
As fast the hours slip away.

What we had planned for, all along,
Can be part of tomorrow's song.
No need to rush...the pressure's gone.
So why...do I...awake at dawn?

Plans?

Gray sky...and ever changing waves
Make moot the problems of my day.

Impossible to still the tides,
I must accept things, come what may.

I must accept...cannot direct
The ever shifting sands...

And yes, the sun caress again
Our constant changing plans.

Gratitude

One star, and just
    the sliver of a moon
Has lit my pathway
    to an open sea

And the horizon,
    dressed in shocking pink
Connects my soul
    to its eternity.

With soon the sun
    like clockwork on its way
I drop on bended knee
    and God, I pray

My gratitude
    for being here right now.
For giving me
    another lovely day!

Colors Of A Storm

Shore birds announce an evening mist
And storm clouds gather o'er my head;

Fore runner of approaching winds
And lo - a threatening rain begins.

The torrents stir an angry sea
And then, as it was meant to be

The sun shone on each curling wave
And best of miracles, it gave

Spread there, before me, end to end,
Out of the sea and back again,

A rainbow – only God had made –
Intensifying every shade

Until the colors seemed to shout
"This is what God – is all about!"

In awe – I watched it fade away
The ending – of a perfect day.

Tranquility

I've roamed the shore
    To pick up shells
        Of every shape and size.

I've talked to birds
    Along the way
        That soar before my eyes.

I've watched a black
    And threat'ning sky
        Turn happy shades of blue

And with it, calm
    The angry sea
        To wash the sands a'new

With salty spray.
    Again, today
        I'm filled with awe that we

Can be so blest
    To be a part
        Of such tranquility!

Sunrise

Like magic,
    all the stars have disappeared
And left the sliver
    of a moon, alone
To light a silver pathway
    to the sea.
(Soft pounds the gentle surf,
    relentlessly)
And here I sit,
    to patiently await
The miracle of sunrise…
    Such a thrill
(I want to shake awake
    those sleeping still.)
Gray clouds appear
    and ever gently now
Become a purple...mauve...
    transparent pink.
The waves from black to silver
    rolling in...
Make very imminent
    the dawn...I think!

Each cloud on the horizon
    rims in gold
And out the sea
    a ball of fire...bold!
It's happening...
    God's miracle
      I say...
        Is break of day!

A Bayou

Have you ever been in a Cyprus swamp?
Come along and I'll take you there...

Where the undergrowth is dank and dark
And the trees are spring-time bare...

Where limbs are draped in Spanish moss
And vines create a maze

Through Cyprus roots, where fowl feed
And the raccoon spend their days...

Where great blue heron build their nest
Mid-stream, in a Cyprus tree

And fuzzy babies seek the edge
To peer at you and me.

Where alligators bask the sun
And watching for their prey...

Have barely moved or blinked an eye
For the entire day.

We drone along through shallow swamp
And bayou...eagerly.

Mysterious the habitants
We're privileged to see.

Don't Tell Me

Lo, don't tell me "There is no God!"
For I've just walked the shore.

I've felt the mighty surging wave
Caress the tired feet,
    And pave with shells
      the sandy shore.

"Lord, toss me up a souvenir!"
Said I, "to carry home"

And two waves hence, a star-fish came.
Within a wave, it came again
    for me...alone
      to own.

No, don't tell me there is no God
While there's a bird to wing...

A puffy cloud, a whisper breeze
To stir the branches of my trees
    and hear...a small boy
      sing!

Vermont

My heart is filled with memories
Of farms and barns of new mown hay,

The fields of corn and herds of cows
And Oh, so much I have to say

Of soaring mountains, ribbon roads
That wind from town to town...

Unspoiled, uncluttered, gentle life...
I treasured every sound...

For there, the hands of time were still
And life, a kindly pace...

Of walls and gardens, verdant green...
Of friends...and love...and grace.

"Upper Michigan"

Storm clouds away
And let the eagle soar.

Gentle breeze
Caress your quiet shore.

In calm of early morn
Bring sun again

Where yesterday
The beat of heavy rain

Erased the footprints
Of a silent deer

And evidence
A prowling cat was near.

Wash well the reeds
That hold the shifting sand

But let the birch
And aging cedar stand.

In friendship, bind
The people of your shore.

Exude tranquility,
Forever more!

Wyoming

Virgin forests
 reach in majesty...
  Each vying
   to be taller
    than the rest.

Blue spruce, among the green
 in varied shades...
  and ponderosa
   feeling
    at their best.

White patch of aspen
 turning now to gold...
  Announce
   approaching winter
    threat of snow

When dainty blooms
 that fringe the winding road
  give way
   a last hurrah
    before they go.

Come – Tour The Rhine

To roam the towns of yesteryear
When first the morning suns appear –
To drink the patchy country-side
Of grape and hops along our ride.

We dream among the vineyards – steep
In awe of where and how they reap.
We view the caves for storing wine,
And with the ghosts of castles dine.

Through France and Germany we dream.
We watch, in awe, the mighty stream
That separates the parapet
From whence nobility were set.

We taste the food of foreign boards
And walk the halls of ancient lords,
Perchance, a bit of lore to glean
Of cypress tree and sword we've seen.

The lights of night along the Rhine
Are but a memory in time
But ever in our thoughts abide
The thrill of foreign country-side.

Holland Dream

So flat the land...so strong the wind
They harness it...for gathering

To work the mill...to grind the grain
To pump the water from the plain

While laughing children run and play
Upon the dykes of yesterday.

The cattle graze the patchwork field
Held not by fence, for on the lea

(and just as far as eye can see)
Canals...divide the scenery...

And shiny windows, framed in lace
Exhibit plants in every space...

While many boats still ply their way
The old canals of yesterday.

The little ducks...the happy faces...
Playing dogs and friendly places...

Fancy foods and always cheese...
Oh, I shall ever dream of these.

An English Dance

They dip and swirl
    They step in tune.

I sit and watch
    Like a buffoon.

They smile, they frown,
    They concentrate.

They glide, and then
    Rejoin their mate.

I agonize
    Quite in advance

I'll not escape
    At least one dance

With Mr. Dapper
    On his way

Across the floor
    To make my day.

We glide, we stride
    And I'm aware

We're center of
    Each English stare.

Victorian Reflection

It was there – it was all there –

The hand-rubbed and loved
    embellishments of yester-year
The ribbons and rosettes of plaster
    on ever-so-ethereal ceilings.
The faceted panels, ornate
    in ribs and scrolls of elegance
Reflecting the warmth
    of antique frosted glass, aglow.

It was all there –

Original hardware of another era.
    Ornate knob-plates, on doors
Polished by the hands of time.
    Warm love walks these rooms –
Antiques settle comfortably
    Amid Persian elegance
        and soft lamp glow.
Enthralled, I gulped it in
    And tucked it in memory –
        For I was its guest!

Artists

Who carves the famous likeness of
A man of great renown

That sensitive creator of
Such figure is profound...

Or painter of such character
In faces he may see

Immortalized on canvas
Shall forever famous be...

Who plucks a string of music and
Creates a symphony

That thrills a world with magic
Surely stirs the heart of me...

But...no appreciation
For posterity...be-lie

The culinary artist, who
Can bake an apple pie!

Restoration

This spacious home
    of olden brick and charm,
In formal garden
    of an era...past

Full glows and echoes
    laughter...here and now.
Its occupants
    replacing pomp at last.

The furniture,
    in keeping with its time
Is polished
    with a tender, loving touch

While floors and glass
    exude the caring hands
And pride...of one
who loves it very much.

The Bird-Bath

Not dreaming, but quite factual
    Reminder of the past,
Today some "purple finch" in awe
    Were shown to take a bath.

The juveniles stood awkwardly,
    Long-legged, at the edge.
Their speckled feathers tightly drawn
    They cocked their little heads.

They stretched their necks in disbelief
    From one side to the other
And watched the splashing antics
    Of their redhead little mother.

"You hop down in - you flap your wings
    You splash with all your might -
You even duck your head a bit
    Sensation of delight."

"No way," said they, "will we display
    Such antics to get clean.
We like us just the way we are!"
    Then mother left the scene;

And gingerly, each one hopped in
    On tippy-toes, at last
While mother, sat up in the tree
    And watched them take their bath.

Reincarnation

When I'm reincarnated,
If I could be a bird,
I'd rise at dawn, play on the lawn.
I'd eat and sing the whole day long
    Sweet songs you'd never heard.

No television all the time.
No need to stay in bed til nine.
No clothes to wash, no phone to ring.
I'd simply sit and eat and sing...
    If I became a bird.

No meals to plan...or grocery shop
Or keep my eye upon the clock...
No bed to make...or floor to mop
Or calendar to have to watch.
    All that would seem absurd.

No car to start, no gas to buy,
When I'd go off...I'd simply fly.
No clothes or shoes to try and fit.
    I'd simply eat and sing and sit.

My one request...of all my friends
Is... fill your feeders, now and then?

Teddy Bears

Oh the cuddles and love, overwhelming
The squish of a Teddy can do!
I don't think he minds if I hug him.
His arms and his legs all askew!

For as he looks up
With his beady-bright eyes
An innocent calmness
He'll send

While he sits on the sofa,
The bed, or the floor…
And he waits…
Til I hug him…again!

I Wait

Repairmen are hard
    For a layman to find…

I've sought quite a few
    In my day…

They're happy to come
    But they won't tell you when

So you wait…and you sit…
    And you pray

For the patience you need
    To be done with the deed.

They bite off more
    Than they can chew…

While they tell you "tomorrow
    For sure they'll be there"

And you sit…and you wait…
    …and you stew!

The Slow Lane

He seems…a step behind me
Be it morning, noon or night.

I turn to ask a question…but
He's stopped to light his pipe!

We may be running tardy
While I push with all my might.

I'm in the car and waiting
But…he has to fetch his pipe!

We've had a lovely dinner…
We've savored every bite

And eagerly await dessert…
My Lord…he's lit his pipe!

A nervous bunch of energy
Am I…but that's all right.

I watch my cool, collected
Darling hubby smoke his pipe!

When life has reached the ebbing
In his cloud of pearly white,

I'm hoping that St. Peter
Lets him…bring along his pipe!

Mother's Sick?

I push her away
And she sits a bit closer.

She leans on my arm, or instead
She sits and she stares

And she shows me she cares
Asking why...am I lying in bed?

She can't understand
When it's time for our walk

Just why Mother is not getting up!
She rolls her brown eyes

And I hear a big sigh
From my sensitive, lovable pup!

The Parson
"1683"

He isn't here.
He never saw this barn,
Yet long ago...his barn
Stood on this ground.

As long ago
He worked this bit of land
And here...his bit
Of history would stand.

Parishioners could fill
His barn...with hay...
And livestock paid
A debt in olden day.

As surely...Parson Capen
Turned this sod;
He led the folk of Topsfield's
Walk...with God.

To Play

A grandson floods in memory
A childhood time that used to be.
A simple game was so much fun
And it included everyone!

A better marble would to win,
A leather pouch to hoard them in,
As I sat down - the other day
With grandson - on the floor to play.

(I'm sure the floor of yesterday
Wasn't quite so far away
Nor, felt it quite so hard to me
As I search in my memory!)

No need to organize a sport –
No uniform or special court.
We'd take a stick – and draw a line –
Play anywhere – at any time.

And no computer ruled the pack
And no one drove us there – and back.
I just suspect the kids today
Don't know what it is like "to play!"

Hats

Some years ago, when hats were "IN"
And ladies dressed...to even shop,

No one would venture through the door
Without a crowning touch on top!

It might be just a bit of veil
Or large and floppy felt she wore

But always part of dressing up
before she hustled through the door

Was, pat her hair and don a hat
And pin it well so it would stay,

Then venture forth to tea...or church
Or maybe the entire day!

Somehow I think we're lacking for
A time to sit and simply chat.

I really think we could look great,
Each one...attired in a hat!

With Love

"Because the Lord is my shepherd
I have everything I need! He lets me
rest in the meadow grass and leads me
beside the quiet streams...He stands
at my very shoulder in failing health.
He helps me do what honors Him most.

Even when walking through the darkness
I will not be afraid, for you are
close beside me, Lord, guarding, guiding
me... all the way.

You feed my soul with your love.
You welcome me as your guest and my
blessings overflow.

Your goodness and unfailing kindness
will be with me all the days of my life
and even afterward, for you fill me
with your love, forever."

"Lord, let everyone I come in contact with
be blest...because of you and me."

"Fill me Lord with the Holy Spirit."

A-MEN

"Thank Thee Lord"

I find the Lord in simplest of song...
And in this realm He holds for me
The sweet, the gentle stirring of a soul.
No complicated words or music bold,
Just gentle, meaningful and not too long
>His song.
I find God in a scattering of flower...
That tells me of His love, His sweetest joy.
The tall, the short, the casting of such hue
And fragrance, overwhelmed with morning dew
And blending every color as a bower
>With His flower.
I find God in a stand of silent trees...
For in each wood, His shelter is profound.
No complicated walk, but simple trail
And yet these trees withstand a mighty gale
Protecting one another, sand and sea
>Each one God's tree.
I find God in the simplest of place...
Ne'er complicate with reams of unknown prose
Unwritten song or calculating prayer!
>God is not there.
Simplicity can meet God face to face
>Within His place.
We praise God in a multitude of ways...
In threads of song, we orchestrate and sing
Returning all the gifts He has bestowed
And in so doing, light another's load.
We thank Thee Lord, for each and every day
>You bless our way!

My Prayer

God, let me live each lovely day
So I may know, that come what may
I've done my best
     To live the way
          You'd want me to!

Just let me know, if I should stray
That I may stop along the way
     At any time
          Of night or day
               And talk to you!   A-MEN

For Courage

Lord God, I come to you with love
And with praise for all I am,
For all I have, for all I love
And for all who love me.
I ask of you the courage
To face each day
With a better understanding
Of changes that come into our lives.
Lord, keep close to me
And help me day by day
To walk taller, fear less
And with your help
Be strong for those around me,
Who may not know you yet.   A-MEN

Day Dreaming

Oh, would that I could cut a dress
　　From skies of pink and blue!

If only fabrics came in such
　　An ever changing hue!

I'd fashion rainbow colors, from
　　The clouds that pass my door

And I'd wear a finer garment than
　　You'd ever seen before!